ENVIRONMENTAL ISSUES

RENEWABLE ENERGY SOURCES

By Emilie Dufresne

KidHaven
PUBLISHING

Published in 2020 by
KidHaven Publishing, an Imprint of Greenhaven Publishing, LLC
353 3rd Avenue
Suite 255
New York, NY 10010

JUN 1 1 2020   3 9082 14206 2952 KL

© 2020 Booklife Publishing

This edition is published by arrangement with Booklife Publishing

Edited by: Kristy Holmes
Designed by: Amy Li

Cataloging-in-Publication Data

Names: Dufresne, Emilie.
Title: Renewable energy sources / Emilie Dufresne.
Description: New York : KidHaven Publishing, 2020. | Series: Environmental issues | Includes glossary and index.
Identifiers: ISBN 9781534530737 (pbk.) | ISBN 9781534530379 (library bound) | ISBN 9781534531697 (6 pack) | ISBN 9781534530614 (ebook)
Subjects: LCSH: Renewable energy sources--Juvenile literature.
Classification: LCC TJ808.2 D847 2020 | DDC 333.79'4--dc23

Printed in the United States of America

CPSIA compliance information: Batch #BS19KL: For further information contact Greenhaven Publishing LLC,
New York, New York at 1-844-317-7404.

Please visit our website, www.greenhavenpublishing.com. For a free color catalog of all our high-quality books, call toll free 1-844-317-7404 or fax 1-844-317-7405.

Words that look like **this** can be found in the glossary on page 24.

CONTENTS

RENEWABLE AND NONRENEWABLE ENERGY

There are two different types of energy that are used to make power. These are renewable and nonrenewable. Renewable energy is energy that we can keep making more of so that it doesn't run out.

THESE WIND TURBINES CREATE RENEWABLE ENERGY.

Nonrenewable energy comes from materials that will eventually run out. Some nonrenewable energy sources include coal and oil.

OIL RIG

WHY DO WE NEED RENEWABLE ENERGY?

We need renewable energy sources for two main reasons. The first reason is that, one day, nonrenewable energy sources will run out.

WITHOUT RENEWABLE ENERGY SOURCES, WE WOULD BE LEFT WITHOUT POWER AND HEAT.

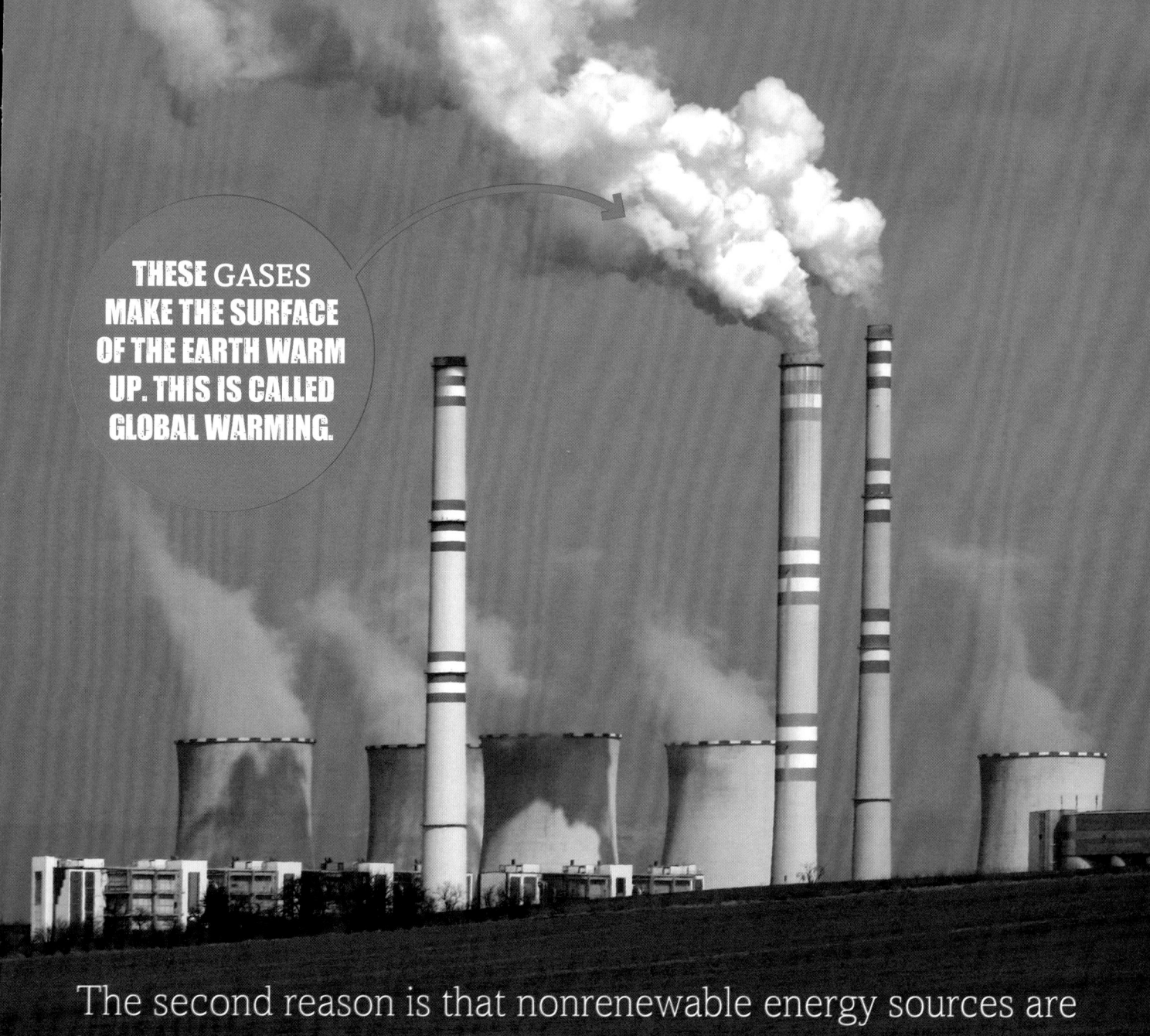

THESE GASES MAKE THE SURFACE OF THE EARTH WARM UP. THIS IS CALLED GLOBAL WARMING.

The second reason is that nonrenewable energy sources are burned to create power. Burning them releases harmful gases into the **environment**.

TYPES OF RENEWABLE ENERGY

Renewable energy uses the world's natural resources to create energy. For example, heat and energy can be collected both from the sun and from deep under Earth's surface.

THIS HEAT CAN BE USED TO HEAT UP HOMES OR MAKE ELECTRICITY.

HYDROELECTRIC POWER PLANT

"HYDRO" MEANS WATER. THIS PLANT USES WATER TO CREATE ELECTRICITY.

The movement of wind and water can also be used to create energy. As water flows through rivers or wind flows through the sky, they can turn turbines which can **generate** energy.

SOLAR POWER

Solar panels can be put anywhere: on the roof of a house, in large fields, or even on the sides of buildings. The panels contain special cells that capture energy from the sun and turn it into heat and electricity.

If we could **harness** all of the energy we get from the sun in one hour, it would be enough to power everything on Earth for a whole year.

WIND POWER

Wind turbines can either be used in a group, called a wind farm, or on their own for a single building. The wind spins the blades. This powers a generator and creates electricity.

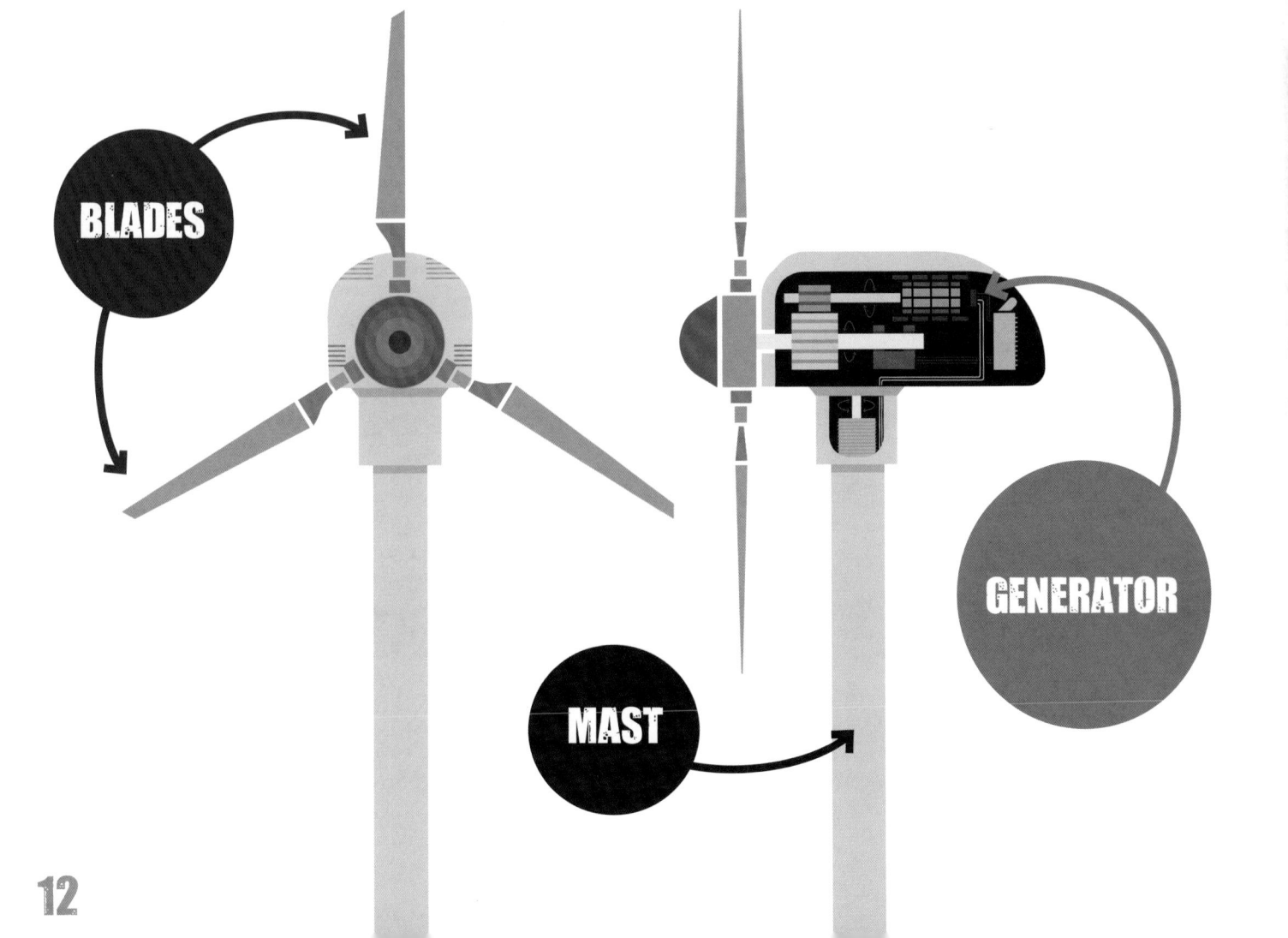

BLADES

MAST

GENERATOR

BLADE BEING REPAIRED

Wind turbines are getting bigger and taller. The bigger a wind turbine is, the more energy it can make. Today, many wind turbines are as tall as the Statue of Liberty.

HYDROPOWER

Hydropower uses the power created by moving water to create electricity. This can be done from rivers flowing downstream, water falling from dams, and the moving tides in the sea.

TIDAL ENERGY FARM

Hydropower is a very **efficient** source of renewable energy.
It can create power all day long and whenever it is needed,
rather than just creating power when it is windy or sunny.

GEOTHERMAL POWER

Geothermal energy is heat that we get from the earth. The earth contains heat from volcanic areas or areas with **geysers**.

"GEO" MEANS "FROM THE EARTH" AND "THERMAL" MEANS "HEAT."

GEOTHERMAL ENERGY PLANT, ICELAND

Geysers and volcanoes heat up rocks and water underground. Pipes can be placed near these hot areas underground. The pipes can send cold water to the warmer areas to heat up.

THE WATER IS WARMED UP AND BROUGHT BACK THROUGH THE PIPES TO HEAT HOMES.

PROBLEMS WITH RENEWABLE ENERGY

Hydroelectric dams can be seen as bad because they damage where fish live and **migrate**. The dams keep the fish from swimming to the rivers they normally go to.

To generate lots of electricity from solar power, lots of solar panels are needed. Often these solar panels are built in large farms. Solar farms take up the space where lots of plants and animals could live.

RENEWABLE ENERGY FACTS

Some of the world's most powerful wind turbines have blades that are bigger than a huge Ferris wheel. The blades are so powerful that just one spin could power some homes for a whole day.

SOLAR PANELS

Lots of **satellites** in the Earth's orbit have solar panels on them. This means they will never run out of energy and can stay in space for many years.

HOW WE CAN HELP

There are lots of things people can do to use renewable energy. Adults can buy electric cars or put solar panels on their homes.

YOU CAN ALWAYS ASK YOUR PARENTS IF THEY USE RENEWABLE ENERGY SOURCES.

GET PEDALING

There are still things you can do to cut down on using nonrenewable energy. If you can, walk or ride your bike to school instead of going in the car.

CUT DOWN ON WASTE

Always remember to recycle anything you can. Lots of harmful gases are released from garbage.

GLOSSARY

efficient   getting the most out of something in the best way possible

environment   the natural world

gases   matter that is air-like and fills any space available

generate   to create or make

geysers   hot springs that shoot out steam and hot water

harness   to make use of

migrate   when animals move from one place to another based on changes in weather

satellites   machines in space that travel around planets, take photographs, and collect and send information

turbines   machines that look similar to fans and are driven by air or water pushing against the blades, making them move

INDEX

24